Lily's Book of
Big Life Lessons

To every little heart dreaming big,
and to all the grown-ups guiding them along the way—
This book is for you. And to my two daughters, Atarah & Amarah, who inspire me daily with their kindness and love—thank you for being the light in my life.

May you always believe in yourself,
choose kindness, and keep learning every step of the journey.

With love and hope,
C Brutus

Dear Parents,

Thank you for sharing Lily's Book of Big Life Lessons with your child. This story aims to spark discussions about crucial values and life skills in a relatable way.

As parents, our role is essential in guiding our children, and this book supports that journey by promoting kindness, courage, and responsibility while building confidence and resilience.

Use this book to initiate conversations, such as:
- "Which lesson is your favorite, and why?"
- "Can you recall a time you were brave or kind?"
- "What does it mean to do the right thing when no one is watching?"

These discussions help children relate lessons to their lives and recognize how their choices impact the world.

Thank you for being a guide and role model. Together, we can nurture thoughtful, kind, and confident individuals.

With gratitude,

C Brutus

Preface

As we grow, life teaches us in little moments—through friendships, challenges, laughter, and even mistakes. Lily's Book of Big Life Lessons was inspired by the idea that children are never too young to start learning about the values that shape us into kind, strong, and thoughtful people.

This book is more than just a collection of lessons; it's a guide to help children navigate the world with confidence and compassion. Each lesson is written in a way that young readers can understand and relate to, with Lily acting as their friendly guide.

Whether it's learning to believe in yourself, showing kindness, or understanding when to say no, these lessons are timeless and universal. They're not just for children—they're for families to read together, discuss, and grow from.

I hope this book sparks meaningful conversations and becomes a treasured resource for building character, empathy, and resilience in young hearts.

Hi there!

My name is Lily, and I have something special to share with you. Life is full of adventures, challenges, and surprises, and along the way, I've learned some important lessons. These lessons aren't just for grown-ups—they're for kids like us too!

Some lessons will make you feel brave, like believing in yourself. Others will remind you to be kind, honest, and patient. There are even lessons about staying safe, like being cautious and learning to say no.

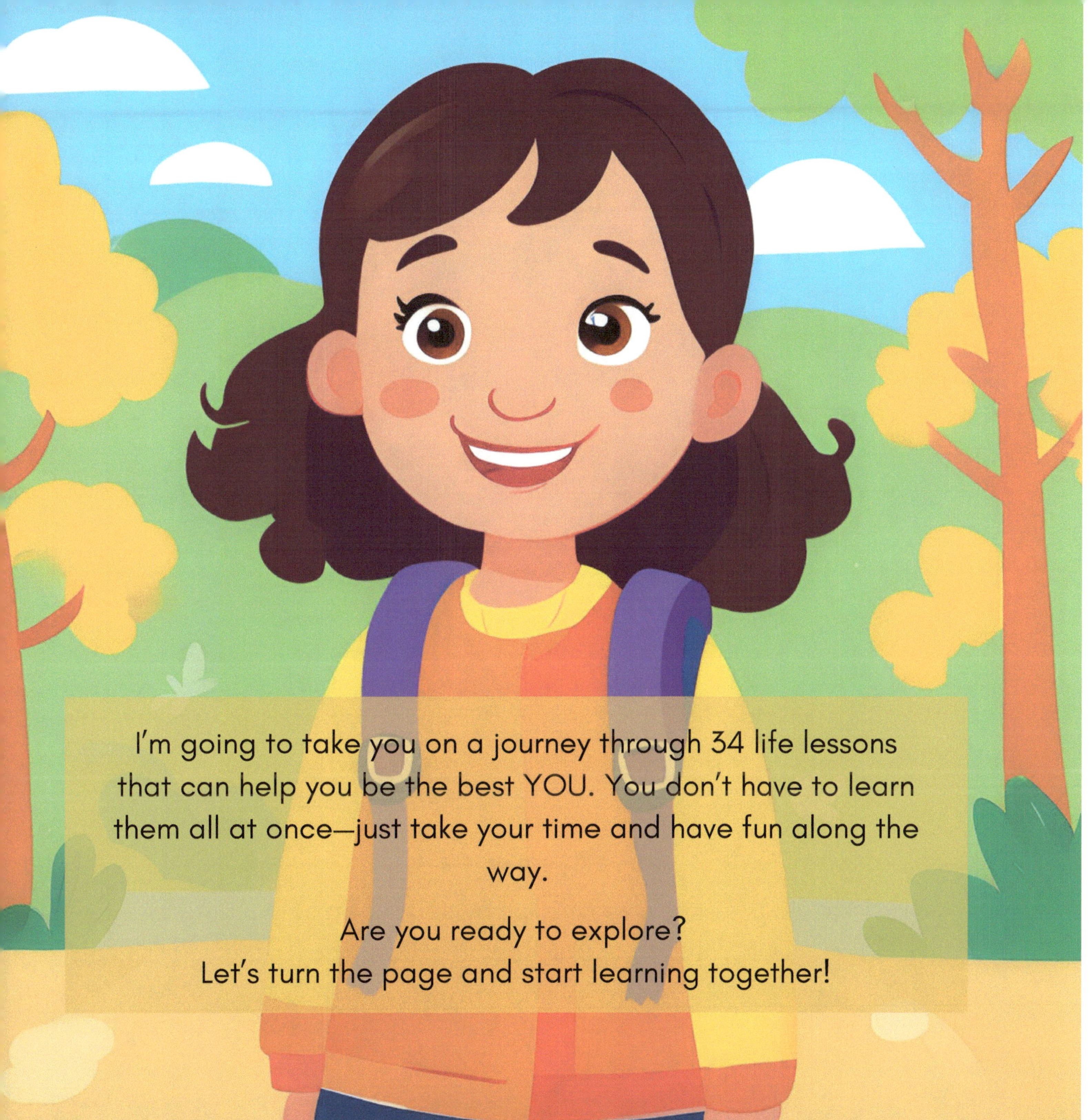
I'm going to take you on a journey through 34 life lessons that can help you be the best YOU. You don't have to learn them all at once—just take your time and have fun along the way.

Are you ready to explore?
Let's turn the page and start learning together!

Believe in Yourself

"You can do it!" That's what I tell myself when something feels hard. Believing in yourself is like having a superpower. It makes you brave and strong!

Be Kind

A smile, a hug, or a helping hand can make someone's day. Being kind is like planting seeds of happiness everywhere you go.

Never Give Up

When I try something new and it's tricky, I remind myself: "Keep going, Lily!" Falling down is okay; getting back up is what matters.

Be Honest

Telling the truth is important, even when it's hard. Honesty makes people trust you, and trust is like a golden treasure.

Learn from Your Mistakes

Sometimes I mess up, like spilling my milk or saying the wrong thing. But mistakes are like teachers—they help us learn and grow!

Be Curious

The world is full of wonders! Ask questions, explore, and never stop learning. Curiosity is like a key that opens new doors.

Be Cautious

It's good to be curious, but I've learned to stay safe by being cautious. I always ask a trusted grown-up before trying something new or going somewhere unfamiliar.

Share with Others

Sharing makes everyone feel included. Whether it's my toys or my time, I love sharing because it makes hearts happy.

Listen Carefully

When my friends talk, I listen. Listening shows you care and helps you understand others better.

Be Patient

Good things take time, like baking cookies or waiting for flowers to bloom. Patience is a special kind of strength.

Treat Others Fairly

Everyone deserves a turn and a chance to shine. Being fair means being a good friend.

Show Gratitude

Saying "thank you" is my favorite way to show how much I appreciate things. Gratitude makes every day feel like a gift.

Stay Positive

Sometimes clouds cover the sun, but it's still shining behind them. Staying positive is like carrying sunshine in your heart.

Be Brave

Trying new things, like meeting new friends or climbing tall slides, can be scary. But being brave means doing it anyway!

Respect Others

Everyone is different, and that's what makes us special. Respecting others' feelings and ideas shows we care.

Take Care of Yourself

Eating healthy food, sleeping well, and exercising are like giving your body a big hug.

Help Those in Need

When someone needs help, even a little bit can make a big difference. Helping others feels good inside!

Keep Promises

When I say, "I'll do it," I try my best to keep my word. Keeping promises builds trust.

Be Yourself

There's only one YOU in the whole wide world, and that's amazing!
Be proud of who you are.

Ask for Help

It's okay to ask for help when you need it. Even superheroes need sidekicks sometimes!

Forgive Quickly

Sometimes people make mistakes that hurt us. Forgiving is like letting go of a heavy backpack—you feel lighter and happier.

Learn to Say No

Sometimes people ask me to do things that don't feel right or that I'm too busy for. It's okay to say "no" kindly. Saying no means taking care of yourself.

Be Careful Who You Trust

Most people are kind, but not everyone is. I've learned to trust people who show me kindness, honesty, and respect. Be careful, and don't trust too quickly.

Do the Right Thing, Even When No One is Looking

One of my favorite lessons is to always do what's right, even if no one sees. It makes me feel proud inside, like a secret smile just for me.

Dream Big

Dream about becoming an astronaut, a chef, and an artist!
Dreams are like stars guiding us to amazing places.

Be a Good Sport

Winning is fun, but playing together is what really matters. Being a good sport makes games more fun for everyone.

Take Breaks

When I feel tired or overwhelmed, I take a deep breath and rest. Breaks help me feel better and stronger.

Be Gentle with Nature

The trees, flowers, and animals need our care. Being gentle with nature makes the world a happier place.

Keep Learning

Every day is a chance to learn something new, like how to whistle or tie my shoes. Learning keeps life exciting!

Celebrate Differences

Some friends like soccer, and some like painting. That's okay! Our differences make life colorful and fun.

Be Grateful for Family

Family is like a warm hug that's always there. I'm thankful for the love and laughter we share.

Spread Joy

A kind word, a joke, or a happy dance can brighten someone's day. Spreading joy is like sharing a little bit of magic.

Love Yourself

Look in the mirror and say, "I love you, myself!" Loving yourself makes your heart happy and strong.

Now you know some important life lessons! Which one is your favorite?

Remember, you don't have to learn them all at once. Take it one step at a time, and you'll grow into the best YOU ever!

My favorite lesson is...

____

____

____

About the Author

I am C Brutus, born in Haiti in October 1992. After moving to the U.S., I balanced my roles as a devoted mother of two and a supportive Navy wife while pursuing education. I work with special education students, demonstrating my commitment to inclusivity. Additionally, I am an author of various children's books, including coloring and activity books, aimed at engaging young minds. I appreciate the support from my customers for my small business.

Thank you!